Angry Rebel

Ned Naggyah

*An angry rebel, a fair maiden,
and the wondrous cross*

TEACH Services, Inc.
PUBLISHING
www.TEACHServices.com

Copyright © 2012 TEACH Services, Inc
ISBN-13: 978-1-57258-927-8 (Paperback)
ISBN-13: 978-1-57258-928-5 (ePub)
ISBN-13: 978-1-57258-929-2 (Kindle/Mobi)

Library of Congress Control Number: 2012946395

Printed in Canada

Published by

TEACH Services, Inc.

P U B L I S H I N G

www.TEACHServices.com

Table of Contents

Introduction

This is the story of a rebel who had no respect for law, order, anything, or anybody. He once desecrated the Bible, disliked Jesus, and hated all Christians until he came face to face with Jesus Christ upon the cross. The battle raged on for two long years. Finally the angry rebel conceded defeat and surrendered all to Jesus. The angry rebel in this book went from being a child of the world to becoming a child of the King.

Chapter 1

Little Boy Introduced to Jesus

My world, as a child, was one of poverty, fear, and anger. My home consisted of a tin shack with wooden shutters and a mud floor. I spent my childhood days playing in our large yard and running around under the weeping willow tree. Even during the difficult times, I enjoyed playing under the huge weeping willow tree.

Our home was owned by my uncle. He lived next door in a large brick house with electricity and a telephone. In those days such items were a luxury, and you were considered rich if you had them. Another wealthy cousin lived a few streets away. When she would visit my uncle and aunt, she often took a shortcut through our yard and would stop to chat with my mother, who often could be found outside washing clothes on a stone slab. My mother would politely invite my cousin into our home, but she would always reply, "Your tin house is too dark for me."

This same dialogue went on week after week. Finally, one day I asked my mother why she bothered to invite my cousin in when her reply was always the same. My mother gently rebuked me and told me to always respect my elders. Ironically, these rich cousins had one son, and when they were getting on in years, they put him in charge of all their financial affairs. In just one year he gambled away every penny. Even their large brick house had to be auctioned off to pay the gambling debts. This once rich family was now left penniless.

Unfortunately, my cousins situation affected us, because my rich uncle who owned our house asked my father to vacate the land by the end of the month so that our cousins could move into the home. By nature my father was a calm and gentle person, but he grew very angry at his brother. He asked him where he would take his wife and children and how he would feed them. Our crop was still growing in the garden. But the cry of my father invoked no pity from my uncle, and we were forced to move.

My elder brother left school sooner to help out with our family's financial situation, and because of this we were able to move to another home with a large garden. The rich cousin who had now become poor moved into the very same tin shack that she said was too dark for her. Years later my rich uncle went bankrupt, and I learned the important lesson that pride goes before a fall.

I was a little boy when I was first introduced to Jesus. Every Sunday afternoon four white missionaries would drive down the dusty road in our village ringing a bell and calling out "Sunday School, Sunday School." We would all run behind their car and gather in an open field where we heard stories of Jesus with the visual aid of felt boards and were taught to sing choruses. The story of Jesus walking on the water was deeply etched in my memory. At the end of the service they would treat us to little stamps with Bible verses and pictures on them, and on special occasions such as Easter they would treat us to hot cross buns and soft drinks.

But the good times were few and far between. In 1949 when I was about six years old, rioting broke out near our village. Hordes of black men went on a rampage torching Indian homes; looting; killing Indian men, women, and children; or raping the women and kidnapping them. It was a time filled with fear.

My mother hid us in the bushes to protect us from these atrocities. I remember her clamping her hands over my mouth to prevent me from screaming, thus drawing attention to the black mobs in the area. But it was impossible to close your ears to the sounds of screaming women and children as they cried out for help.

Finally one day my mother took us away from the danger zone to a place of safety. My father stayed behind to watch over our home. Unfortunately, a gang of black men attacked him and split his skull with a machete, causing him severe head and bodily injuries. He was left in a pool of blood to die. The neighbors who were hiding in the bushes managed to get him to a hospital after his attackers left. When I next saw my father his head and body was heavily swathed in bandages. Although my father recovered from his injuries, he was never the same again.

These horrific events left me frightfully traumatized. I had recurring nightmares where I would wake up bathed in sweat. In my dreams I could hear the tortured screams of women and children. These nightmares did not cease until I became a

Christian many years down the road.

Unfortunately, the government was very slow to respond to the crisis. Even at the tender age of six, anger welled up in me over the mistreatment of my friends and family. I vowed that when I grew up I would kill every black person I came across for what they had done to my father. The embers of hate smoldered in my young heart.

As I grew up and heard more horror stories of how the Indian population had been treated during the riots, my resolve hardened and my hatred increased against the black race.

Chapter 2

A Rebel Joins a Street Gang

I was the only rebel child in my family. My violent temper developed at a very young age, and I could not seem to control it. I was uncontrollable. One day my playmate, who was the same age as myself, angered me so much that, blinded by fury, I threw a rock at him and hit him on the temple, which knocked him to the ground. He lay unconscious. Concerned family members stood around him helplessly. In those days you couldn't call 911. There were no emergency personnel or hospitals nearby. After a while he regained consciousness, and we were buddies again. I was sternly reprimanded for my actions; however, my reasoning was that he provoked me, and I got even. I felt no remorse. This incident gave me a strange feeling of power and dominance, which sent me spiraling down into a world of chaos and violence.

Times were hard, and I left school to work much sooner than most other children.

My father was a poor market gardener who scratched out a living from a patch of land. But somehow our family seemed to multiply faster than his money, and we were ill clothed and unshod. Don't get the wrong idea about my father. He was not lazy or a spendthrift; he was a hardworking and honest man, a devout Hindu who taught us to believe in his religion.

But I didn't care about religion. Rebellion set in at a very young age, and no amount of punishment at home or school could change my destructive course. One teacher commented that there was no hope for me and that I would spend the rest of my life behind prison bars. My long-suffering father could take it no longer and was ready to send me to a reformatory. My mother's pleading gave me a reprieve.

Work brought another world within my reach, a world of new and exciting experiences. I began smoking pot and anything that would make me high. It was during the rock and roll era when stovepipe jeans, leather jackets, and sharp knives were all part of the street gang scene—the scene into which I drifted.

The values of the guys in the gang were distorted. We enjoyed damaging parked cars and public buildings and ripping open bus seats. Street fights against rival gangs soon supplemented these tame activities, which invariably left me nursing terrible injuries. The gang enjoyed crashing social parties and wedding receptions, causing much havoc and unhappiness in the process. I still tremble when I think back on the numerous times death loomed its ugly face at me but I was spared.

The dagger was my constant companion. I practiced for hours until I finally honed my skills at knife throwing. In my world you had to know how to protect yourself, because you never knew what lurked around the corner.

After a night of mind-blowing pot and drugs, the gang was sporting for trouble. We sat around discussing the 1949 riots and its devastating effects. This sent us into a raging fury. At that very moment a black man and his son came down the corrugated road. We were in a foul mood and decided to murder them and dump their bodies in the river. We blocked their way and hurled obscenities and curses upon them. The pair knew they were going to die, and they pleaded for their lives. This enraged us even further.

For some unknown reason their heartfelt pleading touched a core deep within me. I stepped in front of the father and son, shielding them from the group, and told my friends to let them go. My friends' anger was now directed at me. They demanded, "What the (expletive) for? They had no pity on our families. Since when did you become a lover of these blacks."

Things were turning ugly, as I suddenly became the victim. Now my life was at stake. When one's mind is induced by drugs, there is no reasoning power, whether it be friend or foe. There is no honor among thugs; it is each man for himself.

For the first time I unsheathed my dagger and turned it on my friends. I figured that if I was going down I was going to take some of them with me. Then someone had a brilliant idea. "Let's go smoke more pot." The tension quickly eased at the thought of indulging in more drugs. The black man and his son raised their hands in a gesture of thanks and hurried away.

As time passed there started to be more infighting among our gang. We would assemble at a secluded area, which we called "The Hill of Death," and the opposing parties would go to combat without weapons but with no holds barred. There were wild cheers at this bloodletting sport until the loser gave up, battered, bruised, bleeding, and nearly half dead. I had some victories and some losses. Win or lose fighting was one way of releasing my suppressed anger by taking it out on my opponent.

At the end of our battles, I would drag myself home, and my mother would tend to my wounds with some old-fashioned Indian remedies. I would see the anguish on her face as she would say to me, "Why, my son? When will you stop? What drives you on this course of destruction? You remind me of a wild mountain goat."

When I think about it now, I shudder at the sheer savagery of it all. Nights and weekends were spent steeped in drugs and smoking pot. Woe to anyone who crossed our path.

One evening a very unfortunate black woman came our way. We lured her into a field, and the quiet night erupted with the tortured screams of the victim. As a pack of wild dogs at feeding time, they took turns at her. After the incident of the black man and his son, I could not intervene, knowing how fragile my situation could get confronting drug-induced and sex-crazed minds.

As I slowly walked away from the scene into the cold dark night, I felt like a coward. The cold wind that blew across the meadow cleared my drug-saturated mind, but nothing could still the rage and disappointment I felt deep within me.

In my days Hindus were very protective toward their daughters. My older brother was secretly dating a girl, but somehow her family found out. Her father was a big man, and on this day he was standing outside his home as my brother walked down the road. Her father called him over and punched him, knocking him to the ground. Some female relatives of the girl then climbed on top of my brother and punched and scratched him.

I was walking down the road a short distance behind my brother and saw what was happening. I picked up a brick from the side of the road and walked toward her father. He had a smirk on his face and was so distracted watching the drama that he failed to notice me.

I threw the brick at him with all my strength, hitting him squarely on the jaw. I heard a cracking sound, and his eyes rolled back in his head as he collapsed over the picket fence.

I grabbed the women by their hair and

yanked them off my brother who was bleeding profusely. The women screamed even louder when they saw the prostrate form of their relative lying on the ground.

We hurried away from the scene. My brother asked me what had happened. I told him that I had knocked the smirk off the man's face with a brick and most probably broke his jaw. I felt no remorse for what I had done, just an icy cold feeling of anger.

My brother turned and looked at my stony face and said, "I'm sure glad to be your brother and not your enemy."

Chapter 3

Mocking God

Because I did not see a future to my downward spiraling life, I did not fear anyone, not even the devil. Being a Hindu, it upset me that many Hindus were being converted to Christianity, so I desecrated the Bible, disliked Jesus, and hated all Christians.

One evening after the gang got heavily intoxicated, we passed a large tent in which a Christian revival service was in progress. We decided to crash the meeting and have fun mocking these Christians and their God. After noisily taking our seats, we proceeded to punctuate the sermon with raucous "Amens" and "Praise the Lord."

When the preacher invited those wanting special spiritual help to come forward, we all trooped to the front, where he prayed for us in spite of our irreligious attitude. This done, we left the tent, but not before the preacher had pressed a little book into my hand.

Upon waking the next morning, I examined the little book and found that it was a copy of the Christian New Testament. As I stared at the book cupped in my hand, the events of the previous night slowly took focus, leaving me with the strong feeling of fear. I had mocked the Christian God, something I should have never done. For the first time in my life I knew that He was real. So real that I could speak to Him, and I did, saying, "I did the wrong thing last night. I should have never mocked You. I'm sorry." I really felt bad about what I'd done, but I was quick to add, "But I still can't accept You as my God. Maybe someday, but not now!" With that I gave the book away.

I had mocked God, but He was watching out for me, as was evident in a situation I experienced in the court of law.

One day an archenemy of mine, a bully who used his brute strength to intimidate others, crossed my path, and we got into a terrible fight. I had been beaten by him in the past, being nearly pounded into oblivion. So when I met him again I employed every dirty trick I knew as a street fighter, but things did not go as I had planned. Although I avoided the beating, I was arrested and taken to jail while he was taken to the hospital.

Standing in the prisoner's dock, I looked at the judge and the prosecutor who was examining the victim's terrible wounds. My archenemy looked as if he had been hit by a train. I was charged with grievous bodily harm, which carried a minimum sentence of five years imprisonment with hard labor.

I did not have much faith in the justice system of the white man in this apartheid era. For example, if a non-white person killed a white man, they would hang him. On the other hand if a white man killed a non-white man, he would get a six-month suspended sentence.

The prospect of spending all that time in prison did not appeal to me. Prisons are notorious for violence and crime. I knew that if I was sent to prison I would kill someone or be killed. I realized I had come to the end of my journey. All this raced through my mind as I stood gloomily in the prisoner's dock. The evidence against me was overwhelming, and I resigned myself to my fate. Then something strange happened. There was a very elegant stranger in the courthouse that day. Something about him was so uniquely different. He approached the judge, conferred with him, and then left the courtroom.

After that moment the case took a dramatic turn in my favor. The judge's sentence required me to pay a small fine, but other than that I was acquitted of the crime. My heart leapt with joy as I walked out into the bright sunshine. The bizarre outcome of this case puzzled me for many years. Only after I became a Christian did this mystery get solved. After coming to Christ, I realized that the sophisticated stranger had to have been a heavenly appointed counselor who secured my freedom.

Although this experience shook me up, it did not snap me out of the current course I was traveling down, and yet God was still there as was evident in another experience.

It was a balmy night, and I was walking through a dark unlit lane to get to my home on the other side. Normally I was alert to any dangers that lurked around the corner, as my lifestyle did not endear me to many people. But on this night I was preoccupied. I had engaged in some unsavory business that was weighing heavily on my mind.

At that moment an assailant materialized out of nowhere and held me by my shirtfront with one hand. With the other hand he pressed the sharp point of the cold steel knife against my neck. I was momentarily stunned. I knew I was going to die a bloody death. Looking over my assailant's shoulder, I noticed two people enter the dark lane. They were dressed in white shimmering clothes that lit up the darkness. My assailant turned around and saw them too. Instantly, he released me and made a hasty retreat. With my heart pounding, I hurried along to meet my rescuers. I reached the end of the lane, but they had simply vanished. I was rooted to the spot, puzzled and bewildered.

For years this incident invoked a curiosity in me that would not go away. When I became a Christian many years later, I realized that God had been watching over me and had sent His angels to rescue me, even though I was not a Christian.

He spared my life and chose me as a vessel, a worthless sinner, to do His will and bring glory to His name in the years to come.

Chapter 4

Our Life Motto

Living on the wild side of life, I sustained detrimental head injuries that, in later years, caused blinding migraines that rendered me helpless at times. We were in our early twenties, reckless and dangerous. Our motto was "live fast, die young, and have a pretty corpse." Living fast and dying young were easy, but I soon discovered that there is no such thing as a pretty corpse.

By now one of my friends was in prison for dealing drugs; another friend was killed instantly when his car slammed into a tree; another died from collapsed lungs; one friend committed suicide because of problems with his girlfriend; and another had a rare disease that caused him to look like a walking skeleton, hunched over like an old man.

Then my best friend went home one day while his father was at work and found his mother in bed with another man. He was devastated at what he saw, and he con- fided in me. I did not know what advice to give him; my own world was a topsy- turvy one. The only way I knew to solve a problem was with my fists or a knife. I told my friend to stick a knife into his mother's boyfriend. Fortunately, he didn't listen to my advice. But nothing could console him.

Over the next few weeks he slowly with- drew into a shell, and he disappeared for a long while. When I next saw him, he was sitting on the sidewalk eating a half loaf of bread that someone had given him. His hair and beard was long, filthy, and mat- ted. His fingernails were dirty and over- grown. His clothes were tattered and torn, and he only had on one old shoe. I gently spoke to him and called his name, but he just looked at me blankly and went back to eating his bread. I left some money for him and sadly walked away. This once good- looking boy in the prime of his life had completely wasted away, and from what I saw, he had reached a point of no return.

But through all this drama, unknown to me at the time, the God of heaven was pre- serving my life for greater things He had in store for me.

Around this time we moved to another town. Our house was located near a movie theater, which I used to frequent. In the town a blind man, led by his young daughter, went from house to house playing his banjo and singing Indian movie songs. This was his livelihood, and many people gave this very talented man money.

One day he asked the theater owner if he could place a chair at the back of the theater so that he could listen to the songs in the movies and learn to play them.

The wealthy theater owner chided him, "I have three shows a day running to full capacity. I do not have time for your needs; now go away."

The blind man sadly walked away with his daughter. Amazingly, a week later we heard that the very theater owner who had refused to help the blind man had gone completely blind. Sometimes we reap what we sow faster than other times.

Chapter 5

The Hit Squad

My life took a different turn when I left for Durban to accept a new job. Fortunately, I left all my gang friends and most of my bad habits behind me when I moved to this busy port city of South Africa. But old habits are hard to shake. With reckless abandon I carried on with life, knowing that my time would run out the way I lived it, violently.

While in Durban I got involved with a woman, but my instincts kept telling me I was flirting with terrible danger. I was being drawn into a web of intrigue and deception. Being exposed to danger for so many years, I had developed a keen sense of awareness of my surroundings. It was while I was dating this woman that I felt I was being followed, but I could not pinpoint my stalker. I spoke to her about my concerns. She admitted that she was a mobster's mistress but did not love him.

It was at that moment that I knew I was a dead man.

Retribution was swift; the hit squad was on to me. Walking home I heard the whine of a high-powered engine. I turned around in time to see a car speeding behind me. Realizing I was the target, and with only moments to spare, I dived onto the grass and the car sped away. missing me by inches. I knew that there might not be a next time, so I packed my bags and under the cover of darkness escaped to another town.

Often times I pondered about my em-battled life. Would I ever find true peace and happiness? In my new surroundings, I found it hard to break into a new circle of friends, so I spent many hours alone reading. Religious Hindu literature began to interest me, and I enjoyed reviewing the faith my parents had taught me as a child. I studied deeply and devotedly practiced the religion of my parents.

At that time marriage was not on my agenda. With my violent temperament and lifestyle, I knew I would destroy any last-ing relationship. I was like a restless wind with no past, no present, and no future. Then as fate would have it I met a beau-tiful girl. With thick black hair flowing below her waist and flawless skin, her angelic smile disarmed the angry rebel in me. I realized my days of being footloose and fancy-free were fast coming to an end. She captivated my heart. I was captured by her beauty, but our worlds were on a collision course.

Her world was made up of things that were sweet and good; my world was terrifying and was filled with mayhem and chaos. She was like a tender rose blooming at the edge of a desert. I was like the wild desert wind. Would the harsh wind destroy the tender plant? For the first time in my life I felt that there was some meaning to my futile existence. I felt peace and joy in her presence. She was young and innocent. She looked up to me for love and protection. If I wanted a meaningful and lasting relationship, I had to change and control my violent temper. I realized my tender rose must be gently uprooted and placed in a beautiful garden. I had to become the gentle breeze.

After a while I decided to take the plunge, and I asked her to marry me. She said yes, and we began planning our life together. Following the wedding, we embarked on a new journey as husband and wife. Married life was bliss. I enjoyed my role as provider and protector. We did not have much, but when I came home from work, her warm embrace and charming smile dispelled all tiredness. My heart always leapt with joy at seeing her.

However, being married to a beautiful woman had its drawbacks. Being East Indian she wore a sari and a red dot on her forehead to denote that she was married, but this did not deter men from gawking at her, which made me livid with rage. With great effort I controlled myself. I did not want her to discover my violent side. But one day I couldn't take it anymore. We were at a function, and I caught this fellow staring at her. I silently went up to him, jabbed him hard in the ribs, and hissed at him that if he did not stop staring at my wife I would pluck out his eyes and cripple him so badly that he would never look at another woman again. He winced and made a hasty retreat. I should never have felt jealousy—she proved she was a one-man woman—but I was still struggling with the violence of my past.

Many months later we became parents to a beautiful daughter. A few years passed and another beautiful daughter arrived on the scene. We were a happy family and enjoyed our role as parents.

I was moving away from my past, but reminders of my previous life still came back to haunt me. One such area was my dislike of blacks, since I struggled with what they had done to my people. However, I had to face my feelings about the riots since black men and women came to our home seeking chores in the house and garden. My emotions were split concerning them. In one way I pitied them for the way the white government treated and oppressed them; on the other hand I could not forget what they had done to my father. I tried with great difficulty to stay neutral. My wife on the other hand loved all people, regardless of color, creed, or religion. She was born long after the 1949 riots and had not experienced the terrifying situation I had. She paid them much more than the job warranted, fed them, and made parcels of food for them to take home to their children. They loved her and always came back for more work.

Chapter 6

The Wondrous Cross

Our religion was very precious to both of us. I learned to repeat the mantras (holy chants) and spent a lot of time chanting and meditating. During my morning and evening prayers, I would sit in the lotus position and pray with the use of the Hindu rosary. We were also very strict about fasting and the observance of Hindu holy days.

My rising religious fervor made me intolerant of those who were careless about the Hindu faith and tradition. I was especially outspoken against those influenced by Christianity, and I came to dislike Jesus Christ. At times that dislike flared into anger, and I would curse those who mentioned His name in my presence.

By now my wife was pregnant with our third baby. My life centered around my family and our Hindu religion until the events of one remarkable evening. I had completed my prayers, retired to bed, and fallen soundly asleep. Suddenly my sleep was invaded by a most vivid and disturbing dream in which I saw the man Jesus towering above me on a massive wooden cross. His head hung toward His right shoulder. I was awestruck by His beauty and physique. He was the most beautiful person I had ever seen, and I said to Him, "Lord, I didn't know You looked like this." He opened His eyes very slowly. Golden yellow beams, like the headlights of a car, radiated from His eyes and rushed toward me. I was completely engulfed by this light. I couldn't see anymore. I covered my eyes with my hands, shielding myself from the brightness.

Then the dream faded, and I awoke with a strange and yet wonderful excitement. Not able to keep the dream to myself, I gently shook my wife awake and told her what I had experienced. All through the retelling, one question seemed to hurl itself at me, "Why did Jesus appear to me? I am not a Christian!" But the night provided no answer to my question.

Two nights later I had another disturbing dream. In this dream I found myself repeating the words "In the name of the Father, the Son, and the Holy Spirit" again and again. As I awoke the dream became a reality, for these strange words were actually coming from my lips. It was most alarming. Here I was, a dedicated Hindu, repeating Christian prayers instead of the traditional mantras of my own religion. I gently shook my wife awake and told her what I'd experienced.

A third vivid dream followed a few nights later. I was sitting in a room when I felt a strange presence of holiness. I turned around and looked at the opened doorway. I saw a towering, majestic person of ancient times. His robe I could see, but his face was shrouded in a circling mist, and I cried out, "Father Emmanuel." He lifted His huge left hand and blessed me and then disappeared. Who was this Father Emmanuel who left me with a pounding heart while feeling elated? Once again I gently shook my wife awake and told her what I'd experienced.

A few months later, my wife gave me the most beautiful birthday present—a lovely baby daughter was born on my birthday.

After having the three dreams I could not pray as a Hindu anymore. Every time I sat to meditate and pray with the rosary, Jesus would invade my meditation, and I would discontinue my prayers. I did not want Jesus in my life; I was born a Hindu and had no desire to change. And thus for two years the battle raged in my heart. The power of Jesus pulled me toward Him while another force pushed me away from Him. Deeply puzzled and in urgent need of some satisfying answers, I visited many churches. They were unanimous in telling me that their God was calling me to become a Christian. They explained to me that Jesus is the Son of God; that the Father, Son, and Holy Spirit are the Trinity; and that Emmanuel means "God with us."

But I did not want to believe. How could Someone whom I had disliked so much want me to become one of His followers? That did not sound right at all. I was happy being a Hindu and was not going to change.

But as time passed I started to fall in love with this tender, beautiful, loving Jesus. One day as I sat in the living room thinking deeply about my present spiritual life, which seemed to be in tatters, everything suddenly came into focus. My mind went back to the Christian camp meeting twenty years earlier during which I'd insulted God and then half-heartedly promised Him I would follow Him some day. Jesus remembered the feeble promise I had made when I had held His Word in my hand and said, "Maybe someday, but not now." It seemed that a great burden was lifted from me. I simply said, "Lord, I can't fight You anymore. You win." I knew right then that I must follow Him.

But what about the rest of my family? Fortunately, God had been preparing their hearts, and when I asked my wife and three daughters if we should remain Hindus or become Christians, the vote for Jesus was overwhelming. With everyone committed to the same thing, the next question was which church to attend. There were so many churches, and they all seemed different. My wife suggested that we attend a church where some neighbors went on Saturdays.

I thought these people were quite strange. I was under the impression that it was common knowledge that Sunday was a church day. When I used to drive to the market on Saturday mornings, I would see these people standing at the bus stop with Bibles in their hand, and I would often give them a ride to the church. I would chuckle to myself because they stuck out as a sore thumb going to church on a Saturday. I told my wife we would attend any church except this peculiar Saturday church.

But my search for the "real" church was overpowering. I wanted to do everything acceptable in God's sight. We prayed and asked God to lead us to His church. That very night I had another vivid dream. I saw these Saturday worshippers sitting around a table with a Bible in their midst. I immediately awoke and realized that the Bible was God's book and that my neighbors were God's people. The following Saturday my family and I attended the Verulam Seventh-day Adventist Church. We were warmly welcomed. We found the worship to be wholesome and enjoyable and at the same time full of reverence. In due course we were baptized, and thirty years later we are still regular, churchgoing, happy Christians.

We are thankful for the love of Jesus, which successfully penetrated the gloomy stronghold of traditional religion and led us into the light of Christianity. I feel humbled by a mighty God who called a worthless sinner into His fold, and I want to live for Him today and every day for the rest of my life.

Chapter 7

Learning the Ways of Jesus

After we accepted the Lord and started attending church, we asked the pastor and a few elders to come to our home and remove the Hindu idols and other items of worship we had prayed to. After removing the idols, they blessed our home through a prayer session. First we prayed upstairs, and then we proceeded downstairs where we had kept our Hindu shrine.

It was downstairs that we also had a veranda where I had my gardening shoes, my daughter's tricycle, and an old window burglar guard placed neatly against the wall. It was a calm day, but as the pastor prayed a loud wind was heard in the veranda, and we could hear things being thrown around. On investigating, we found the gardening shoes, the tricycle, and the burglar guard had been thrown across the veranda. Satan was not happy when Jesus evicted him from our home, and he displayed his anger. But our home was filled with the peace of Jesus.

Thankful that our home was free of idols, we continued to learn all we could about our new faith. I enjoyed studying the Bible, but when it came to the study of tithes and offerings, I became distressed. The reason being was that the company I worked for was just starting off. My boss promised me that as the company grew I would grow with it, and I looked forward to a bright future. But right now I worked hard and put in many hours without overtime pay. Our family budget was tight. That weekend I prayed and explained the situation to the Lord. I told Him that I wanted to be faithful but that our budget did not allow me to tithe.

That very Monday morning my boss called me into his office and thanked me for my hard work. He told me the company was growing and doing well, and he gave me a 10 percent increase in my salary. My heart leapt with joy. I went home and told my wife that the Lord was paying His own tithes. I never looked back, and I faithfully rendered my tithes. My boss kept his word. He helped me with the down payment for our home, and he gave me his mother's car. My salary increased in leaps and bounds. At the end of the year, I received my salary with a 100 percent bonus. The Lord was true to His promise in Malachi 3:10, and He provided for us beyond our expectations. I loved my job and worked for the company for twenty-two years before immigrating to Canada.

As we learned and grew in our newfound faith, we desired to be baptized and to publicly express our decision to follow Jesus. Our baptism was most memorable and mysterious. It was a beautiful sunny Sabbath afternoon with not a cloud in the sky. My wife and I got into our baptismal gowns and were getting ready to be baptized by the conference president when it suddenly grew very dark. Peals of thunder and flashes of lightning could be seen and heard followed by a heavy torrential downpour. We proceeded with the baptism, and as soon as we came up out of the water, the thunder, lightning, and rain ceased as quickly as it had started. The sun shone brightly once more.

I have never forgotten the strange weather that day. All I can conclude is that all of heaven must have been rejoicing with us to see my wife and I, sinners in need of a Savior, take the plunge in the cleansing wave. And the Most High God manifested His majesty power by this unusual display through nature.

Like all new Christians, I still had much to learn in my walk with Christ. This story will give you a glimpse into the early struggles and decisions I faced in my faith. I had two cars. Because it was a time of recession, maintaining two cars was not feasible, so I decided to sell one. I advertised it in the paper, but no one called. After a week I took it to the Lord in prayer and asked Him to send a buyer. That very afternoon I received a call, the man came by to see the car, we settled on a price, and he paid me in cash.

I was excited about the turn of events and was enjoying the feeling of a thick wad of notes warming my pocket, but my wife put a damper on my happiness. She said, "Don't forget the Lord's tithe." I reasoned that I had not worked for the money so there was no need to render tithe to the Lord. I had only sold a car. I found many excuses not to render my tithe, and I felt justified.

I went to bed that night with a smile on my face, but that smile quickly vanished. I was only half asleep when the whole house shook to its very foundation and a voice thundered across the room like rushing water: "Why has thou robbed me?" I lay there paralyzed in fear; my heart pounding against my chest. I thought I was going to die. When I recovered enough, I feebly managed to murmur, "I am sorry, Lord."

I couldn't sleep the rest of the night, and the next morning I took out the money and counted out more than the 10 percent just to be on the safe side. From that time forth I was very careful when it came to the Lord's holy money.

My family has never let me forget this incident, and they often ask me, "Whatever made you think you could rob the Lord and get away with it?" It still fascinates me because there are billions of people on the planet who cheat the Lord, but He took the time to point out my sin. That experience taught me that the Lord knows everything and sees everything. Nothing is hidden from Him.

A few months later a calm and majestic voice spoke to me in a dream, saying, "Of all thine increases thou shall tithe." I sat bolt upright in bed, trying to think of where I had gone wrong, and then it dawned on me. We had an investment that was earning a considerable amount of interest that

I needed to pay tithe on. I thanked the Lord for the friendly reminder and did the right thing first thing in the morning.

In addition to taking care of us financially, God also protected us from the problems of this world. Here is one example. After visiting my mother who lived in our old hometown, we prayed for the Lord to give us safe traveling mercies. On our way back home, I heard a loud noise coming from the engine compartment. I stopped the car on the side of the highway. I could hear the sound of gushing water, and I noticed that the heat gauge had risen to the "H" mark. I knew something was drastically wrong. I got out of the car to investigate.

I could see water flowing from under the car. I opened the hood and with some old rags I opened the radiator cap. A lot of pressure had built up, but the radiator was empty. I looked behind the radiator, and I could see some water still pouring out from a hole about three inches in diameter at the bottom of the radiator core. We were in big trouble. In those days there were no cell phones or roadside assistance. I looked on both sides of the highway, and all I could see were open fields for miles and miles. There wasn't even a house in sight where we could go get help. We were stuck in the middle of nowhere between two cities, the other drivers were too nervous to stop and render assistance, and I couldn't blame them.

I got back into the car and explained our predicament to my family. I grabbed the container of water from the trunk and we bowed our heads and prayed. "Lord, we are stuck. Our families don't know where we are, but You know our situation. I am going to pour water into the now empty radiator, and we leave the rest up to You."

I poured the cold water into the hot radiator even though it was not a good idea as it could crack the engine block. I was fearful to look at the bottom of the radiator because I expected the water to pour out through the open hole at the bottom, but to my amazement, the water filled to the top. I closed the radiator cap, shut the hood, got behind the wheel, and started the car. My family started to sing praises to God.

The heat gauge was still at the "H" mark, and the engine could blow at any time, but we knew God was in charge. Then miraculously the heat gauge started to drop down until it settled on the "N" mark. The engine was performing normally. I told my family to enjoy the ride because the Lord was taking us home. I merged into the fast lane, and when we arrived home, it was dark. Safely home, we fell on our knees and thanked the Lord.

At first light the next morning I opened the hood and unscrewed the radiator cap. The water was at the very top, not a drop had been lost. I looked behind the radiator core. I tried to feel where the hole was supposed to be, but there was no hole. I drove the car for a few weeks before deciding to change the radiator. I asked the mechanic to show me the old radiator, but there was no hole—it was completely sealed by God.

God fixes broken homes, broken marriages, broken lives, and broken radiators! He provides for our needs, both big and small.

Chapter 8

Working for the Lord

Soon I was the head elder of the church, my wife was the head deaconess and treasurer, and my daughters were active in Sabbath School and in the youth programs.

Every day I spent time reading my Bible. I was fascinated by the Holy Spirit, but I wanted proof of His existence, so I prayed and asked the Lord to show me the third person of the Godhead who was a mystery to me. *Who is He Lord, and how does He impact our lives?* I prayed.

That very night I had a vivid dream. The church was full of worshippers when a powerful wind blew into the building, and the whole church shook from the force of a mighty earthquake. The wind rushed from the back of the church forward with a great humming sound and with great speed. It seemed that He was reading the thoughts and minds of all the worshippers. In a few moments it was over, and a relative calm settled over the church.

I awoke knowing that God had answered my prayer. As a result of that dream, whenever I enter a church, I am constantly reminded of the mighty power of the Holy Spirit. With great reverence I worship my Creator. The Lord said, "Reverence my sanctuary."

At this time our congregation did not have a church building. We worshipped at a Methodist Church whose doors opened onto an open market. The noise was so terrible that even when we closed the doors the noise could still be heard inside, thus making worship difficult. From there we moved to another hall that faced a pub. Then we moved to a school classroom that was so small that the women and children had to sit in the classroom while the men sat outside. The pastor would stand at the doorway and preach.

I questioned the Lord, telling Him we were His children and should not have to worship Him as nomads, moving from one place to another. As church members we constantly fasted and prayed, asking God for a church of our own.

One night I had a dream in which a majestic voice commanded me, "Build Me a church." I immediately awoke and pondered this strange request from the Lord. I said, "Lord, who am I to build You a church, and how do I build You a church?" But there was no answer to my questions.

The next Sabbath we had a visitor—a young white gentleman. Because of the apartheid laws, each racial group worshipped in their own community. There was very little interracial mixing. To see a strange white man in our midst was somewhat odd. He sat outside the classroom with the men. At the end of the service, he approached me and asked, "Why do you worship under such conditions?"

I told him, "We have a plot of land, but we cannot build on it. We have made various requests to the borough to erect a welfare center/church building, but our requests have been turned down time and again citing a certain bylaw concerning the servitude and boundary that cannot be changed."

The young man asked to give him all the information concerning the building plot, and we did. I had never seen him before, and I never saw him again. In about three months the borough wrote to us and said the bylaw had been rescinded, and we had permission to erect a welfare center/

church building. We just had to submit our plans.

The conference helped us financially, but we had to cover the shortfall. We had cards printed with our welfare organization number, and the church members went out and solicited funds.

My family and I were passionate about God's church and His instructions to me. We collected the highest amount from soliciting funds door to door, which wasn't easy. People had fenced in properties because of the high crime rate, and many kept vicious dogs who were trained to bite or kill. But God promised He would send His angels to watch over us, and He did. With this promise we went to people's homes. In all the years we went Ingathering (gathering money for feeding the poor and needy) and collected funds for the building project, not one dog wagged its tail, sniffed, growled, barked, or bit us. To the owners' amazement, the dogs would completely disappear from the scene or the Lord would cause them to fall into a deep sleep. Today a magnificent church and welfare center stands as a monument to God's majestic power.

My family and I had a passion for the Lord's work. We wanted to share the gospel

with everyone, even if it took us to un-
charted places that exposed my family to
danger. We were a unit operating under
God's protection. Our goal every Sabbath
afternoon was to distribute fifty *Signs of
the Times* magazines to homes in our community. One such place we worked was
a shantytown known for its drug addicts,
drug dealers, and prostitutes. The dregs of
society lived there. But we felt they were
God's children who had been led astray by
the devil, and they needed to know that
Jesus loved them and that there was hope.

One sunny Sabbath afternoon we stood
in the yard of a family who was sitting on
the veranda telling them about a loving
Savior. Suddenly a stocky, muscular man
in shorts and a vest with his arms covered
in tattoos began shouting and cursing
at us. I took the situation in at a glance;
he was heading straight toward me like a
runaway train, but fearlessly I stood my
ground, remembering a saying from my
younger days, "Fear no man nor the devil."

I continued talking to the family. The
man came and stood next to me, breathing
heavily. In my younger days I could have
ripped him with my dagger just for cursing
at me. But I do not carry a dagger anymore.
Instead, I carry a much more formidable

weapon of defense—a two-edged sword, the sword of the Spirit, God's Holy Bible. The man listened to me as I expounded on God's Word. Then he ever so gently tapped me on my shoulder. I turned around, and he asked very politely, "Will you pray for me?" I gladly prayed for him.

When you are about the Lord's business, never fear when you tread on the devil's playground, defy him because God will send His holy angels to protect you. We proved God's protection time and time again.

My wife and I experienced God's power on another occasion when we were out giving Bible studies, something we used to do a lot. We had left our children at home in the Lord's care and gone to study with this family. After the study as we were driving home, we both noticed a massive opened book in the sky. It was only 8:30 p.m., but it was very dark out and there wasn't any traffic on the road. The book was lit up with many lights darting upon it. It was a most spectacular sight to behold. It stayed in our view until we reached home. We still do not know the meaning of this wonderful experience, but it was awesome, majestic, and a little frightening.

Chapter 9

Witnessing at Work

By now my boss had two companies on the same floor. One was a data processing company, and the other was a building information service, which I worked for. In the data processing section there were many Christians, Hindus, and Muslims. At lunch we would play darts for prizes. In my younger days as a street fighter, I mastered the art of knife throwing. Thus I became an expert at the game of darts, winning many office prizes.

One day I was playing against a Muslim man who generally disliked Christians. As he threw the darts, he would repeat "In the name of the Father, the Son, and the Holy Spirit" again and again. I warned him not to take God's name in vain, but he paid no heed. By now I was seething with anger— nobody insults my God and gets away with it. Christian principles forbade me from bashing his head against the wall. With great difficulty I controlled myself as he continued to blaspheme the name of God.

Sadly, that weekend he and his wife were in a head-on collision with another car. His pregnant wife was critically injured and lost the baby. He never again took God's name in vain.

In this same company there was a Muslim fanatic who continually harassed the Hindus and Christians, causing a lot of discomfort and distress in the office. His supervisor was also a Muslim who turned a deaf ear to everyone's complaints. Being the most senior employee, some of my coworkers came to me for support. I obtained an English version of the Quran and studied it. When I had gleaned enough information, I called the fanatic into my office and asked him why he was harassing the Christians. I opened the Quran to his shock and amazement and pointed out quotations from his holy book concerning Jesus. Here are some of the things I pointed out to him from the Quran. (Sura = Chapter / Isa = Jesus)

Quran's view concerning Old Testaments prophets

- Given to Musa (Moses)
  – Sura 2:50–52

- Is a blest admonition
  – Sura 21:48–50
- No better source of judgment or guidance – Sura 5:43–48
- The Quran confirms Moses writings and should not be doubted – Sura 32:23–25

What the Quran says about the gospel

- Gospel given to Isa – Sura 57:27
- Believe all, do not divide it – Sura 42:12–15
- To reject it is to be thrown into hell – Sura 42:70–72
- Follow former scriptures – Sura 20:133
- Quran confirms what was sent before, the Bible – Sura 10:37, 38; 35:30
- If in doubt, ask those who have read the Bible – Sura 10:92–94; 21:7
- Must believe in Bible equally with the Quran – Sura 4:135
- Do not dispute or debate with the people of the book; believe both have one God – Sura 29:46

Attitude commanded by the Muslims toward the Christians

- If in doubt, ask them and have confidence in them – Sura 5:82
- Allowed to marry Christians but not heathens – Sura 5:4, 5

Titles given to Jesus in the Quran

- "The word" – Sura 4:172; 3:45
- "A sign" – Sura 21:91; 43:61
- "Messiah" – Sura 3:45
- "Holy boy," "His prophet," "Owner of the book," "Word of God," "Illustrious"

Role the Quran assigns to John the Baptist

- "Yahya" (John) was to confess to a Word from Allah or testify of Jesus. He was to be a leader in spiritual matters, even a prophet – Sura 3:39

Miracles or "Signs" the Quran ascribes to Jesus

- He would be born of a virgin – Sura 3:44–53; 19:15–30
- He would heal the blind and lepers

and resurrect the dead. This would be a sign – Sura 3:49
- Christ is sinless according to the Quran whereas other prophets have sinned – Sura 19:19
- Noah asked for forgiveness – Sura 71:28
- So did Abraham – Sura 14:40, 41
- Even Mohammed is told to ask for forgiveness – Sura 47:18, 19
- Death and resurrection prophesied by Isa – Sura 19:32-33; 3:54, 55; 4:157, 158

The day of judgment

- A day of doom is coming which will consume all nature. The Lord will come with a shout to raise the dead from their sleep. All will ascend unto the Lord for judgment – Sura 22:1; 81:17; 82:1–52; 3:54, 55
- On that great day all classes will be brought before the throne of God, no sins can be hidden, and a man will be a witness against himself. The good will receive their reward and the wicked will be punished – Sura 69:12–19 (13–20); 75:4–30; 22:15–17
- Hell will be a very real experience

– Sura 18:98–105; 14:47–51; 22:18–22; 47:14, 15

Reward of the righteous in a newly created earth

- The second coming is described – Sura 4:158; 39:67–73
- Eden restored – Sura 14:47, 48; 21:101–105; 19:59–64; 47:11–15

After this discussion with this Muslim man, he never again mocked his Christian or Hindu coworkers. Instead, he became rather subdued.

Chapter 10

Bible Truths

I am so grateful that through study and prayer God has showed me His biblical truths. Armed with God's Word, I have been able to share with others the joys of living according to God's precepts.

When my wife and I were looking for a church, the Lord showed me that the seventh day (Saturday) is the Sabbath, the Christian day of worship. But being of a curious mind I researched and studied the topic as to why the majority of Christians worshipped on Sunday, the first day of the week. I read many books and explored the topic extensively. I also read the Bible slowly and diligently from Genesis to Revelation— since then I've read it many times over and still do.

God speaks of the seventh day 126 times in the Old Testament and sixty-two times in the New Testament. The first day of the week (Sunday) is mentioned only eight times in the New Testament. Most Christians believe that Sunday is the Sabbath day of worship, and they use this text to support the evidence—Acts 20:7 talks about Paul and his friends gathering for a Saturday evening get-together that lasted until the first day of the week. He preached until midnight and then traveled to Assos on Sunday morning (verse 13).

But nothing is mentioned of a change of the seventh-day Sabbath to Sunday. Look at Acts 17:2: "And Paul, as his manner was, went in unto them, and three sabbath days reasoned with them out of the scriptures." Jesus, as our example, also attended church on Saturday, the seventh day (Luke 4:16).

Through the years I have spoken to many Sunday ministers. Some agree that the seventh day, Saturday, is the Christian day of worship, but it seems if they pursued this subject they would lose their jobs. Pilate was afraid of losing his job, too, although Jesus stood before him an innocent man. He washed his hands of Jesus. Some ministers believe the Ten Commandments, with the seventh-day Sabbath in the heart of it, was nailed to the cross. Thus we're living under grace and not under the law. Unfortunately, their belief is in error, for they do not understand the scriptures and the law of God.

As with some of today's ministers, the leaders of Israel did not understand the law of God. On one occasion they dragged a terror-stricken woman before Jesus, accusing her of violating the seventh commandment, which states that "thou shalt not commit adultery." They said to Jesus, "Now Moses in the law commanded us, that such should be stoned: but what sayest thou?" (John 8:5).

In my reading of the scriptures the Lord only physically wrote things down twice: the Ten Commandments on tablets of stone and the guilty secrets of the leaders in the dust. And Jesus said to them, "He that is without sin among you, let him first cast a stone at her" (verse 7). One by one they stole away with bowed heads and down cast eyes. Jesus arose looking at the woman and said "Woman, where are those thine accusers? hath no man condemned thee? She said, No man, Lord. And Jesus said unto her, Neither do I condemn thee: go, and sin no more" (verses 10, 11).

She came condemned under the law, but Jesus sent her away under grace. But we cannot forget that He still pointed her to the law. So what is sin? "Whosoever committeth sin transgresseth the law: for sin is the transgression of the law" (1 John 3:4).

By keeping the law alone one cannot be saved, but only by the precious blood of Jesus. But the law is an integral part of the Christian belief system; it is God's guidelines for all humanity. Let us hear the conclusion of the whole matter: "Fear God, and keep his commandments: for this is the whole duty of man" (Eccl. 12:13).

Where some people get confused is between the distinction of the moral law of God (the Ten Commandments) and the ceremonial law. Look carefully at the difference in the two. The one with animal sacrifices was nailed to the cross; the other will stand forever.

Ten Commandments

1. Is called the "royal law" (James 2:8)
2. Was spoken by God (Deut. 4:12, 13)
3. Was written with the finger of God (Exod. 31:18)
4. Was placed in the ark (Exod. 40:20; Heb. 9:4)
5. Is to stand forever and ever (Ps. 111:7, 8)
6. Was not destroyed by Christ (Matt. 5:17, 18)

Ceremonial Law

1. Is called the law contained in ordinances (Eph. 2:15)
2. Was spoken by Moses (Lev. 1:1–3)
3. Was written by Moses in a book (2 Chron. 35:12)
4. Was placed in the side of the ark (Deut. 31:24–26)
5. Was nailed to the cross (Col. 2:14)
6. Was abolished by Christ (Eph. 2:15)

The two great commandments are "love the Lord thy God with all thy heart, and with all thy soul, ... and with all thy mind; and thy neighbour as thyself" (Luke 10:27). God's Ten Commandments are hanging on these two. The first four tell us how to love God with all our heart (have no other gods, not worship images, not take God's name in vain, and remember His Sabbath day to keep it holy). The last six deal with loving our neighbor as ourselves (honoring our parents, not killing, not committing adultery, not stealing, not lying, not coveting).

Many people believe the Ten Commandments did not exist until given at Mount Sinai. They believe that the commandments were given specifically for the Jewish people and never intended for the Gentiles or Christians.

We will let the Word of God defend itself on this vital question by examining closely God's attitude toward the violation of His precepts before Sinai. Did the Lord have a different standard for His people before the days of Moses? Did He change the rules of Christian living after the first advent? Do we serve a changeable God?

God's Definition of Sin

- Sin is the breaking of the law (1 John 3:4).
- Sin could never be defined without the law (Rom. 3:20).
- We would never be guilty of transgression if the law did not exist (Rom. 4:15).
- Paul would never have known sin "but by the law" (Rom. 7:7).
- When we violate one, we violate all ten (James 2:9–11).

The Law Before Sinai

- Adam could not have sinned if there had been no law to govern his actions (Isa. 43:27).
- Abraham received a blessing because he kept God's commandments (Gen. 26:4, 5).

First Commandment

- If the law was not in existence, how did Jacob know that God disapproved of idols? Before going to Bethel, the first commandment was to be obeyed (Gen. 35:2–4).
- Abraham's father served "other gods," which is a violation of the first commandment (Josh. 24:2).

Second Commandment

- Laban, Jacob's father-in-law, had images. If the second commandment was not binding, then it was perfectly all right to have idols, and Jacob should not have buried them by the oak tree in Shechem before going to Bethel (Gen. 31:19).

Third Commandment

- What was the measuring rule of wickedness in the days of Noah if the third commandment was not in effect and the people were not conversant with it? (Gen. 6:5).
- If there was not a law by which to measure profanity, then how could Esau be charged with being a "profane person"? (Heb. 12:16).

Fourth Commandment

- This commandment was given in the Garden of Eden before there were any Jews on the earth (Gen. 2:1–3).
- It was "made for man" regardless of the period in which we might live, whether B.C. or A.D. (Mark 2:27, 28).
- This experience took place before the law was written. The Lord tested their obedience to the Ten Commandments by their proper observance of the Sabbath, even before the Ten Commandments were officially written and given to the people (Exod. 16:4, 5).
- God wrought a threefold miracle each week for forty years to teach the people the sacredness of His holy day and how it should be observed (Exod. 16:21–30).

Fifth Commandment

- If there was no commandment to honor your father and mother, then Jacob's sons did not commit any wrong by deceiving their father and falsifying to him (Gen. 37:28–35).
- Joseph's brothers acknowledged their wicked deed. They called it

"trespass," "sin," and "evil," and they entreated Joseph to forgive them (Gen. 50:15–17).

- The New Testament, recording the event, says it was "envy" that led Joseph's brothers to do what they did (Acts 7:9). Were they guilty of sin? "Where no law is, there is no transgression" (Rom. 4:15). Therefore, the law was in existence in their day, and they were guilty of violating not only the fifth but also the sixth, ninth, and tenth precepts.

Sixth Commandment

- Cain was guilty of fratricide, but did he commit sin? If there was no law against murder, then was it a crime to kill his brother (Gen. 4:8). The Lord indicted him and measured out punishment for his crime (verses 9–13).
- Cain was a lawbreaker and will be excluded from heaven (1 John 3:12–15).

Seventh Commandment

- Here again we have the assurance that the law was taught; otherwise, how could Joseph know that is was a "sin" to commit adultery? (Gen. 39:7–9).

Eighth Commandment

- Jacob stole the blessing that belonged to his brother. While he repented of the injustice wrought against his brother, he suffered the penalty for his violation of the law by having to flee from home and, in later years, witnessing the same traits in his own sons (Gen. 27:35, 36).

Ninth Commandment

- Jacob practiced deception and falsehood. He could have done it with impunity if there was not a commandment that prohibited such a course (Gen. 27:17–24).

Tenth Commandment

- When the woman "saw," she "took." Eve coveted that which belonged to God before she "took" it. Did she sin in wanting the fruit upon which there was a prohibition? How could she if there was no law against coveting? (Gen. 3:6).

We can clearly see from this study that not only were the Ten Commandments in existence before Sinai, but they have been in force down through the ages. Those who have received Jesus as their Savior will be obedient (John 14:15; Heb. 5:9).

As I have discussed with people, obedience to the law means obedience to the whole law—all ten commandments. Of course, for most people the fourth commandment is the hardest to observe because it goes against mainstream Christian denominations.

When discussing the Sabbath I point out these thoughts. The sun was the main god of the heathen world even as far back as ancient Babylon. Since they worshipped the sun on Sunday, it was much easier for pagans to join the church if Christians met on the same day. It worked well. Pagans flocked in by the multitudes. Satan's plan of compromise and a counterfeit Sabbath was bearing fruit. Many true-hearted loyal Christians were alarmed. They questioned the leaders as to why they had tampered with the law of God. The church leaders had a ready answer. The people were told they were worshipping on Sunday because Jesus rose from the dead on that day.

Then Emperor Constantine became a

Christian. The Roman government was getting shaky, so he wanted to unite the sun worshipping pagans, Christians, and the Roman Empire as never before. In AD 321 Constantine, yielding to the suggestion of church leaders, passed the first Sunday law. "Let all the judges and town people, and the occupation of all trades rest on the venerable day of the Sun" (*The Great Controversy*, p. 679).

So who changed the Sabbath? Here's a bombshell. The Catholic authorities proclaim, "'The Bible says, "Remember that thou keep holy the Sabbath day." The Catholic Church says, No! By my divine power I abolish the Sabbath day, and command you to keep the first day of the week. And lo, the entire civilized world bows down in reverent obedience to the command of the holy Catholic Church'" (Father C. Enright, C. S. S. R. of the Redemptoral College, Kansas City, Mo., June, 1893, as appeared in *History of the Sabbath* by John Nevins Andrews, p. 802).

"Had she not such power she could not have done that which all modern religionists agree with her, she could not have substituted the observance of Sunday the first day of the week, for the observance of Saturday, a change for which there is no

Scriptural authority" (Stephen Keenan, *A Doctrinal Catechism*, p. 174).

Then consider this statement: "'The Catholic church,' declared Cardinal Gibbons, 'by virtue of her divine mission changed the day from Saturday to Sunday'" (*Catholic Mirror,* September 23, 1983). The Council of Laodicea (AD 364) facilitated changing the day of worship from Saturday to Sunday (*The Converts Catechism of Catholic Doctrine,* 3rd ed., p. 50).

Cardinal Gibbons in *The Faith of our Fathers* said, "But you may read the Bible from Genesis to Revelation, and you will not find a single line authorizing the sanctification of Sunday" (p. 89).

Jesus said, "But in vain they do worship me, teaching for doctrines the commandments of men" (Matt. 15:9). And God said in Revelation 18:4, "Come out of her, my people, that ye be not partakers of her sins, and that ye receive not of her plagues."

It's God's last call to all born-again believers to separate themselves from any organization that is not obeying all His commandments. Dear reader, when Jesus pronounces the words in Revelation 22:11, 12—"He that is unjust, let him be unjust still: and he which is filthy, let him be filthy still: and he that is righteous, let him be righteous still: and he that is holy, let him be holy still. And, behold, I come quickly; and my reward is with me, to give every man according as his work shall be"— probation is forever closed for all humankind. One is either saved or lost. Time is running out for this old planet earth, and Jesus beckons you to be part of God's true church.

May He say about us: "Here is the patience of the saints: here are they that keep the commandments of God, and the faith of Jesus" (Rev. 14:12).

The devil will not be happy if you choose to follow Christ. But fear not! The devil is a defeated foe, and his final demise is fast approaching. Pride and self-exaltation led to Lucifer's downfall, and those same traits trap people today. The Bible best sums it up: "Thou was perfect in thy ways from the day that thou was created, till iniquity was found in thee.... Thine heart was lifted up because of thy beauty, thou hast corrupted thy wisdom by reason of thy brightness" (Ezek. 28:15, 17).

"For thou hast said in thine heart, I will ascend into heaven, I will exalt my throne above the stars of God: I will sit also upon the mount of the congregation, in the sides of the north: I will ascend above the heights of the clouds; I will be like the most High" (Isa. 14:13, 14).

Instead of seeking to make God his maker supreme, Lucifer sowed discord among the other angels until the arch-rebel and all his sympathizers (one third of the angels) were banished from heaven. To this day, they continue to sow seeds of discord. And through their masterful work of deception, they lead many to reject God's commandments, which will result in eternal damnation.

But the Lord assures us in Luke 12:32, "Fear not, little flock; for it is your Father's good pleasure to give you the kingdom."

Because the lovely Jesus shed His precious blood for me on the cross of Calvary, I choose, by the grace of God, to follow Him all the way. I urge you to keep all His commandments, including His seventh-day Sabbath. Remember, "blessed are they that do his commandments, that they may have right to the tree of life, and may enter in through the gates into the city" (Rev. 22:14).

Chapter 11

Angel on a Lonely Road

It had not rained for nearly three years. The drought was severe, and the dams were running dry. The people could not wash or bathe because of the lack of water. We were fortunate; my wife's cousin had a country store and also farmed. They had a borehole and always supplied us with water, which we shared with our neighbors.

Then the heavens opened up and it rained nonstop for many days, which caused severe damage to the roads and bridges. The flash flooding washed huge boulders into many homes, killing the occupants.

Even though water was now available, the purification system at the dam could not be operated yet. But we couldn't wait for the water because we were out. So one night after praying and asking the Lord to protect us, we drove to my wife's cousin's home. As we drove along the lonely dark country road, which had sugar cane plantations on either side, a man suddenly emerged and stood in the middle of the road with his hand raised in a gesture to stop. This made me nervous. I put on my high beams. In the bright light I could clearly see the man. He had such a kind face, so I stopped the car. I lowered the window, and he warned us that in the middle of the road ahead was a huge crater from the heavy rains. He told me to go along the grassy area in order to bypass the crater. I thanked him and did as he instructed. I could vaguely make out the outline of the huge hole in the middle of the road as I slowly drove by.

If it had not been for this kind gentleman, I would have driven right into the crater, and we all could have been killed. It peaked our curiosity as to who the man was? There were no houses nearby and no cars parked at the side of the road. Then it struck us like a bolt of lightning. It was raining, and he wasn't even getting wet. The Lord had sent His angel to warn us of impending danger that lay in our path.

Chapter 12

Moving to Canada

The political climate in South Africa was changing. I looked at my children and realized that there was not much of a future for them in South Africa. God had blessed us financially, but I was willing to give up everything to move to a more stable country that offered peace and security to my family.

Around this time there was an advertisement in the local paper for a printer in New Zealand. I was elated, I met all of the qualifications for the job, so I applied for the position. I prayed daily that the Lord would open a way, but many months later when I inquired about the status of my application, I was told they had not received it. I was discouraged and upset with God. I told Him that this was an opportunity for Him to get us out of the country, and He had let me down.

When God closes one door, we often fail

to see when He opens another. My wife kept insisting I call the Canadian embassy, for she had heard that Canada was a beautiful and safe country. I kept putting it off, for I knew it was futile as not many people immigrate to Canada from South Africa. The requirements are very stringent. After weeks of stalling, I finally called the Canadian Embassy. After filling out many forms, we fasted and prayed without ceasing. A date and time was set for an interview with an embassy official. One of the prerequisites was to present a police clearance certificate. We had our fingerprints taken at the local police station and awaited the results. I was discouraged and downcast because I had criminal records that would not sit favorably with the embassy official, and I felt that my application would be turned down. I was told that criminal records in South Africa were never destroyed because the government suspected everyone of being a terrorist, especially if you were non-white.

I pleaded with the Lord, telling Him that He had brought us so far just to be turned down because of my past life. The day before our interview the Lord, in a vivid dream, impressed me not to discuss politics with the embassy official. I was still nervous about the police clearance certificate. The morning of the interview I received a letter from the government. With trembling fingers, I opened the letter. With shock and amazement, I read the brief letter. "To whom it may concern, our records show no criminal activities on the above mentioned person." I breathed a huge sigh of relief and thanked the Lord for this miracle.

Then it was off to the interview at which the embassy official asked many questions and tried to draw me into talking about politics. I followed the Lord's leading and did not engage in discussing politics.

It usually takes twenty-four to thirty-six months to process an application, but God was good to us. We were scheduled to land in beautiful Canada within seven months of our application being approved.

We started to sell everything and were busy packing our bags. But where should we settle? We wanted God to lead us. In another dream a majestic voice said, "Go to Montreal." We did not know where Montreal was. There was no Internet in those days. I searched the library for information on Canada. Because our government did not want us to know how freely people lived in most parts of the world, the information in the library represented Canada as a snowy country with polar bears. We thought there was twelve months of snow.

That Sabbath morning a visitor came to our church. I had never seen him before, nor after, but he said to me, "Brother Ned, I heard you are immigrating to Canada. I have relatives in Montreal." He gave me the address and phone number. So off we flew to Montreal.

Once settled, we began looking for a church family. One evening my wife and I were discussing plans to buy a secondhand car to use on Sabbaths to go to church. The Lord was listening to our conversation, and in a dream that very night a voice said, "Do not buy a secondhand car." The next morning I thanked the Lord for His advice and we leased a new car.

As we looked for an East Indian church, we soon discovered that the majority of the churches were predominantly black. In the beginning it was a bit hard to adapt to a mixed congregation, but we fully integrated with our new church family, and past misconceptions disappeared. These were God's people too. We were greeted with hugs and genuine love every Sabbath morning, and it warmed our hearts. The church members are now as close as family. I thank

God for removing all traces of hatred, dislike, and distrust from me toward these beautiful people.

Chapter 13

The Rock of My Salvation

I used to suffer from constant migraine headaches caused by head injuries I received during my youth. Unfortunately, the severity of the pain rendered me into a state of helplessness and depression. After one of these attacks, I dreamed I was walking past a graveyard where the darkness was very intense. A strong wind was trying to push me backward. I was fearful and kept shouting, "Jesus, help me." Suddenly the graveyard disappeared, and I was surrounded by a blinding brightness and a majestic voice said, "Look unto the Lord, the rock of your salvation." I awoke with a wonderful feeling of peace.

I took many medications to try and control the migraine attacks. But one night in a dream a voice said, "Do not take those strong medications." I harkened to the

Lord's voice, and never again did I suffer with migraine attacks.

I was thrilled to be free from the migraines. God had once again touched my life in a concrete way. I decided to publish my conversion story, "A Love That Won't Let Go," in a church magazine that was distributed to many countries around the world. Some publishers paid me as a token of thanks. About a year later I had a vivid dream. I was in the heavenly courts standing before holy beings. The beauty and brightness of this place shone brighter than the noonday sun. In the background I could faintly see the outline of two holy figures that I figured must have been the Father and Son. The holy beings questioned me politely.

"Do you share your testimony?"

I answered yes.

"Did you have it published?"

I answered yes.

"Did you get paid for it?"

I answered yes, but I quickly added that I did not take the money but gave it all away to the mission field.

I then awoke with a strange feeling of peace that I have never experienced before. When I realized I was back on this gloomy earth, I quickly shut my eyes and hoped

this beautiful dream could go on forever.
The Lord gave me a little taste of heaven.

Chapter 14

Serving Others, Serving God

In Montreal my wife followed her life-long dream by opening an East Indian restaurant, which she ran quite successfully by herself. It was a thriving business, and at times a bit overwhelming with its sudden success even though she closed from Friday sunset to Saturday sunset to observe the Lord's Sabbath. She finally sold the restaurant at a handsome profit after six years of hard work and long hours.

After the sale of the business I had a dream in which I was bathing and caring for an elderly gentleman. I awoke in a state of shock and amazement as this was below my dignity. I had never done this before. But I humbled myself and followed the Lord's leading. My wife accompanied me as we both took a nurse's aid course that prepared us to help care for Alzheimer's patients and seniors with disabilities.

When I had this dream "Uncle Hughie" was active and was still driving old ladies to church. But what he did not know was that in the next few months he would be struck with Alzheimer's, and God loved him so much that he was preparing me to care for him. I registered with an agency that sent me to various private nursing homes and hospitals on an on-call basis to provide care for the sick and elderly. I was constantly watching out for the man in my dream. With so many nursing homes and hospitals, it seemed like a daunting task to find this gentleman. But I had faith in God that we would eventually connect, and we did.

In the beginning I was a bit skeptical about what God was putting me through. This was an Irish gentleman who was nearly 6 foot 2 inches. He had been a gentle giant who never uttered a swear word and who made food baskets for the poor and needy. But the disease turned his world upside down, and he became something he was not. He became very violent; he screamed constantly, swore like a trooper, and lashed out at me all the time. He had to be restrained in bed or whenever I gave him a shower. But with patience and tender loving care, I fed and saw to his every need because he was a child of God who I was appointed to care for.

I asked his niece who was in charge of all his affairs if I could work privately for the family. She agreed and paid me a good salary. Uncle Hughie eventually trusted me and stopped swearing and lashing out at me. He realized I was his friend and was there to care for him. I cared for him as I would my father for twelve long years, and he eventually died in my arms. I was grief stricken. I cannot wait to see him on the resurrection morning. After all these years, his niece, without fail, sends me a thank-you gift every birthday, Easter, and Christmas. This family still remains close to our hearts.

With all this experience we decided to open a foster home. We now care for young men with autism, providing a safe and secure home for them. Some days are very challenging, but with patience, love, and care they overcome their anxieties and fears.

Chapter 15

Two Powerful Dreams

One night after I had prayed and retired to bed, I had a vivid dream in which my wife and I were walking along a huge swollen river we could not cross. Suddenly the water stopped flowing, and only a trickle of water was on the riverbed. My wife and I crossed safely to the other side. I then awoke with a start. Where had the water gone? I could not understand the dream. The children of Israel came to the river Jordan, which was overflowing. God miraculously stopped the flow, and the Israelites crossed over safely.

The next night I had another vivid dream. I saw Jesus rising out of a lake of miry clay bound with chains. He was covered with clay from head to foot, and His garments were soiled. As He arose the chains broke off and the miry clay fell off Him. He stood above the lake, pure and holy. His robe was white as snow, and His face shone with glory. I heard a voice above Him say, "Nothing can keep a holy God down." I gazed upon the unparalleled beauty and purity of the Lord, and He gazed back at me. His gaze penetrated my very soul. No matter how far I moved away from Him, His eyes were upon me. I was the focus of His love.

I could not understand the meaning of these dreams. But in the weeks to come things became clearer. The Lord was preparing me for the fiery trial that was awaiting me around the corner and assuring me of His love and grace.

Being a nature lover, I relaxed in my garden after these dreams, enjoying the tranquility and beauty all around me. The rich foliage of brightly colored flowers and the many varieties of roses in full bloom comforted me. It seemed that the Divine hand had painted each petal with love and precision. I listened to the birds flitting from tree to tree chirping merrily. I gazed upon the vast expanse of the clear blue sky with a cloud dotted here and there. Truly our Creator had spared no effort in creating such magnificent beauty and splendor.

A few days later, my peaceful existence was shattered and my world came crashing down. As I lay drowsily on a hospital stretcher after my gastroscopy on July 31, 2009, the reality of what was happening slowly came into focus. In the distance I could hear the doctor explaining that my symptoms were due to a stage III adeno-carcinoma esophageal tumor. Over the last four months I had experienced severe heartburn, difficulty swallowing, and I had lost thirty pounds. With faith, courage, and hope I faced the terrible onslaught. I was in shock but calmly accepted my fate; my life was in God's hands.

My tumor was so large that it obstructed food from entering the stomach. By God's grace, the cancer cells had only spread to lymph nodes around the tumor. The surgery would involve removing one-third of the esophagus, two-thirds of the stomach, and the affected lymph nodes. Because of the length and potential complications associated with this type of surgery, I was told that I would be in the Intensive Care Unit following the procedure. Esophageal cancer is usually diagnosed at a late stage, therefore, increasing the risk of lymph node involvement and metastasis. The chance of survival is only 25 percent.

The plan seemed simple: three cycles of chemotherapy followed by surgery and ending with another three cycles of chemotherapy. A peripherally inserted central catheter (PICC) line was inserted in my left arm for chemotherapy. My treatment plan was aggressive. For each cycle I would receive two types of intravenous chemotherapy over a course of several hours at the clinic and would leave with the third chemotherapy continuous infusion bag that would last for a week. The side effects left me weak and helpless. I had low blood levels, lack of appetite, painful sores in my mouth, hair loss, nausea and vomiting, extreme fatigue, and even my nail beds turned blue. I became most anguished when my vision became blurry and I couldn't read from the Word of God.

Days were spent completely out of focus. I couldn't even pray or remember a single Bible text. Being a Christian for more than thirty years, I felt blessed to know my Lord, study His Word, and commune with Him daily, but this was unreal and frightening to me. I felt the devil shake my wasted body as a rag doll, but I would not let him shake my faith in Jesus.

On November 10, 2009, I went in for surgery knowing that my family and the entire church were praying for me. Just before the anesthetic took effect, I prayed, "Lord, if I make it through this, it will be a miracle. If not, Lord, remember me when You come on that great day in the clouds of glory. Please take care of my family."

The next thing I remember was being wheeled to a surgical unit with a chest tube, a nasogastric tube, an epidural, and multiple intravenous medications attached to my arm. The hands of the Great Physician were on me, and the surgery was a success. Every test, X-ray, and vital sign reading came back normal—a bed in the intensive care unit was not needed.

With all the intravenous medication infusing through my veins, my days on the unit were spent in a haze. Everything seemed to be happening so fast. Health care professionals would come in and poke and prod me. I could see them speaking but couldn't understand what they were saying. I was overwhelmed. My family was with me every day, but I longed for the familiarity of home.

On day nine following my surgery, I was discharged and eagerly anticipated being at home with my family. The oral pain medications were too strong for my now reduced stomach, and I would double over with cramps. However, without the medication, the pain from the incision site was excruciating. Breathing was an effort.

A few weeks later I started my second round of chemotherapy. The hair on my eyebrows and eyelashes fell off, my once full beard was now patches of whiskers, my eyes were sunken and my cheeks hollow. I was a walking skeleton. I looked and felt as if I was dead. I was discouraged.

I was told to eat foods that would speed up the healing process. How? My mouth once again developed sores. I couldn't eat or drink, and even if I wanted to, I didn't have the energy to even pick up a spoon. I felt myself wasting away. My wife tirelessly and effortlessly did everything she could to help me. I felt useless. Daily injections of Heparin (prevents blood clots) and Neupogen (immune system booster) ran through my body as I felt my life spiraling out of control. I was miserable and felt as if I was dying a slow painful death. My blood sugar and blood pressure levels were so low that I couldn't get up without falling. My family would help me to sit outside to get some sun and fresh air.

I tried to connect with God through nature, but my mind was incapable of grasping any form of reality. The gulf between God and myself seemed to be widening; I could feel the terrible isolation. In my confused mind, I tried to find answers to the chain of events leading to my present predicament. I was drifting in and out of reality. Through my pain and suffering, I tried to seek the Lord, but heaven was silent. All through my life, through many trials, I felt the hand of God guiding and protecting me, but now my heart was breaking. My God whom I loved and trusted seemed to have forsaken me. My cry of anguish was, "Where are you, Lord?"

Day after day, night after night, there was no relief in sight. In my delirious state I could feel the forces of death and its icy cold fingers pressing down upon me. I felt myself falling into an abyss, and I realized I had come to my journey's end. Just when everything seemed lost, I was suddenly prompted by a strange and powerful force to summon every ounce of my strength and get down on the knees. With tears streaming down my face, I managed to utter just three words, "Jesus, help me." With feeble hands and in desperation, I reached out to Jesus. Even death was not going to separate me from my Savior.

Then I felt a strange feeling of peace come over me. The fog lifted, my mind was clearer, and as the days passed my vision improved. I was able to pray and read from God's holy Word. The icy cold fingers of death seemed to recede into the distance. Two PET scans, six months apart, revealed no evidence of cancer in my body. I knew then by the grace of God that I had cheated death: "O death, where is thy sting when there is power in the blood of the Lamb?" Victory in Jesus is mine. My faith was tested to its limits, but my Lord delivered me.

Chapter 16

The Cancer Returns

In May 2011, after almost a year and a half in remission, a mass appeared on my CT scan, and spots on my lungs were seen on my PET scan, resulting in a diagnosis of incurable stage IV cancer.

In my distress I wrote a letter to the Lord:

> *My dearest Lord,*
>
> *With tears and a breaking heart, I write this letter to you. I battled the curse of cancer. I went through excruciating pain and untold suffering. Then for a while You healed me.*
>
> *Now the curse has returned. I am putting up a brave front for the sake of my longsuffering family, but inside I am petrified and paralyzed with fear of the pain and suffering I have to endure once again. WHY, MY LORD?*
>
> *Lord, I did not come looking for You, but You sought me out, and You*

found me in the rubble of sin. In Your love letter You said, "I have called thee by thy name, thou art mine." You brought me out of darkness into your marvelous light. You showed me great and wonderful things of heavenly beings and holy angels. You saved me from certain death on numerous occasions. By Your mighty hand You brought us to this beautiful country, even when everybody said it was impossible.

For nearly thirty years we had this beautiful relationship. We were always frank with one another. I have to admit that although Your love was true and pure, I sometimes betrayed You. But I always came running back to You knowing full well that I could not live without You. I was always overjoyed whenever You forgave me and embraced me in Your loving arms.

So tell me, Lord, when did Your love for me wax cold? I am facing the onslaught of the silent killer cancer for the second time. I call on Your name, but I am met with silence. What have I done, Lord, to deserve Your wrath?

I am tired and weary, and my pleading for a complete healing goes unanswered. If my holding Your Word in my hands and this frail and ravaged body on bended knees is an abhorrence to You, then I pray let me perish and disappear from Your sight. Life is not worth living without You.

Lord, I could bravely face the fires of hell, but what is gut-wrenching and heartbreaking is this wide gulf between us, feeling that You have turned Your face away from me. I am like a reed shaken in the wind.

Lord, in the final analysis I leave it up to You to decide how this love story ends. But I know with my last breath I will still praise You and die loving You.

WHY? Because I have never known of such a great love.

I love You and miss You,
Ned

Though I felt abandoned and out of sheer desperation wrote this letter, I knew there was no other hope but in the Lord, so I fiercely clung to Him. Through this storm of life, my faith was tossed as a little boat on the angry ocean, but my anchor was grounded firm and deep in the Savior's love. God is in charge of my life.

New treatment was ordered. My daily prayer was just to make it through the day. My mind became cloudy again, my appetite decreased, and my weight plummeted.

My intestines became inflamed from the capsules, which caused agonizing pain, and once again I found myself admitted to the hospital with a dangerously low white blood cell count. Since the side effects outweighed the benefits, I debated whether I should continue with the treatment plan. I took this to the Lord, and I decided to discontinue the chemotherapy.

Around this time a church member told us about a Seventh-day Adventist lifestyle center in Colorado called Eden Valley. They specialize in holistic healing of many health issues, including cancer. Once again, my dear family and church members fasted and prayed for me, and I decided to do the eighteen-day program. The lifestyle center was in a valley surrounded by majestic mountains, and once again I was surrounded by God's beauty. I was assigned a doctor and given an individual treatment plan of a vegan diet, fever baths, massages, Russian sauna, hot and cold showers, intravenous Vitamin C, hyperbaric treatments, doctor visits, and blood tests. It was hard being away from home for such a long time, but the staff at Eden Valley made me feel as if I was a part of their family. Prayer was a focal point of my stay, and with love and compassion I was given my treatments. Through their support and encouragement, I was able to keep up with my schedule. Walking became easier, my appetite slowly increased, my mind seemed clearer, and I started to feel like my old self again.

Two weeks after returning home, my oncologist ordered another PET scan, which showed that the tumors in my lungs had miraculously disappeared and the esophageal tumor has shrunk in size by almost a centimeter. I was reminded of the text in Jeremiah 29:11: "For I know the thoughts that I think toward you, saith the LORD ..."

His grace is sufficient for me. As I look out at my garden, which is being covered with fresh snow, I once again marvel at God's creation. If each snowflake is so beautiful in its own individuality, how much more precious are we in God's sight? With a grateful heart I want to shout for the world to hear, "Lord, Thou art good, Thou art kind, and Thou art merciful. All praise, glory, and honor belongs to You, Lord, for Thou art the greatest. Amen!"

Chapter 17

The Bible Is Life

As a Christian I've experienced joys and trials. We are not exempt from pain and suffering, but we have to look beyond this world for what God has in store for us even if death overtakes us.

The following Bible studies strengthened my faith when I was in dire straits, such as fighting cancer. I hope these studies will help you grasp these Bible truths so that you can march on to victory with renewed strength and vigor. With your eyes focused steadfastly on the Savior, you will be able to face life's challenges.

The State of the Dead

Popular Christian beliefs state that when a good person dies they go to heaven and a bad person goes to hell forever. This is not a Bible teaching, although Satan has convinced many people that it is.

Although I lived recklessly in my

younger years, the uncertainty of death and the hereafter did scare me. I studied and practiced Hinduism; however, I did not believe in the concept of reincarnation or the endless cycle of birth and death. It did not make any sense to my probing mind. When my parents died, it dawned on me that I would never see them again. I loved them and wished I could make amends for all the heartache I had caused them. I knew with finality that I had to live with remorse and guilt.

When I became a Christian, I discovered that death is not the ultimate end of life—we shall live again. This is what the Bible says about death.

At death the body goes back to dust; the spirit returns to God who gave it (Eccl. 12:7). This spirit that returns to God is not some entity which is capable of a conscious existence apart from the body, but it is the breath of life (James 2:26), which God gave to us to make us a living, conscious personality (Gen. 2:7). At death that life passes into God's hands for safe-keeping until the resurrection.

The righteous do not go to heaven until the coming of Jesus Christ at the last day (1 Thess. 4:16, 17). All life after death depends on the resurrection (1 Thess. 2:19;

John 14:3). Without the resurrection, the good people who have died would perish (1 Cor. 15:16-18). This could not be true if they went to heaven when they died. If the righteous went to heaven when they died, there would be no need of a resurrection. And there would be no reason for Christ to come back to this earth the second time to gather His saints if they had already gone to heaven at the time of their death (John 14:3). If the wicked go to hell at their death and the righteous to heaven, there is no need of a judgment day at the end of time or for Christ to come to reward every man according to his works (Matt. 16:27; Rev. 22:12). This idea of a person going to hell or heaven at death destroys the Bible doctrine of the resurrection, the coming of Christ, and the judgment at the last day. There is no text in the Bible that, when rightly interpreted, teaches that people go to hell or heaven at death, because the Bible does not contradict its own teachings.

All go to one place at death, and that one place is the grave, where everyone turns to dust again (Eccl. 3:20). The Bible never speaks of the soul or spirit going out of the body at death to maintain, or to become capable of maintaining, a conscious existence somewhere else (Job 30:23; John :28, 29).

Eight times the Bible speaks of the soul as going into the grave (Acts 2:31; Job 33:18–30; Ps. 30:3; 89:48; and Isa. 38:17).

When a man dies, his soul is unconscious until the resurrection (Ps. 146:3, 4). If the righteous went to heaven when they died, they would certainly be praising God now, but this text says that the dead praise not the Lord (Ps. 115:17). Also, the dead do not know anything about what takes place on the earth after they die, because they are unconscious. In the Bible, death is called a sleep fifty-four times. Thus we understand that the dead are unconscious, just as a person is unconscious who is in a deep sleep. The breath of life from God made Adam a living soul, a conscious being, and when that breath of life was taken away at his death, it left him as a dead soul, an unconscious being, until the resurrection when that breath of life or spirit will be put back into him again.

The dead do not know anything (Eccl. 9:5, 6). When a Christian dies, the next moment, as far as his or her sensations are concerned, he or she is with Christ. The lapse of time between a Christian's death and Jesus' second coming, the glorious resurrection day, will seem as an instant. To the righteous who have died, it will seem but the next moment after they close their eyes in death when they awake to be with their blessed Savior forever. The first righteous person who died will awaken and stand in Christ's presence at the same time as the last person who dies. To each, the elapsed time between death and the resurrection will seem but a moment.

I look forward to meeting my parents at this great reunion.

The Seven Last Plagues

Many Christians believe that the seven last plagues in the Bible are just symbolic; on the contrary, they are a reality that will surely happen just prior to Christ's second coming. God will pour out His wrath without mixture by sending on the disobedient seven terrible plagues just before Christ appears at the last day (Rev 14:10; 15:1).

Revelation 16 provides us information about the plagues. The first plague will be a terrible sore on all the millions of people who have the mark of the beast on their forehead or in their hand. Under the second plague the sea will turn to blood. Under the third plague the rivers and fountains, the source of our drinking water, will be turned to blood, and for a time the disobedient will have nothing but blood to drink. This will be like the first plague that came on the Egyptians when their water was turned to blood for seven days (Exod. 7:17–25).

Under the fourth plague the sun will scorch the earth with terrible heat. Under the fifth plague will come a darkness that will be felt. Under the sixth plague the devil's three generals—the dragon, the beast, and the false prophet—will attempt to marshal the whole world to fight against God in the battle of the great day of God. Under the seventh plague great hailstones will fall, weighing a talent each, which according to our system of weights is fifty-seven pounds. Nothing like this ever has happened; so it is clearly in the future.

They will come in one prophetic day, which represents a year (Rev. 18:8). When the time comes under the seventh plague for the mountains and islands to be moved out of their places by that last mighty earthquake, then Christ will appear through the opening heavens (Rev. 6:14–17; 15:17–20).

During the time when these plagues are being poured out, Jesus Christ, our High Priest and Mediator, will no longer plead the merits of His shed blood for sinners (Rev. 15:5–8). During the time of these plagues, there will be no forgiveness for sin. We must turn to God now to receive forgiveness and cleansing from every sin.

Before the plagues begin to fall, every person's case will have been decided forever (Rev. 22:11, 12). Christ will pronounce this decree of Revelation 22:11 at the close of His intercessory and mediatory work. He will cease to plead for sinners as our High Priest. Then the first plague of God's unmixed wrath will fall upon the disobedient. These scriptures make it plain that the seven last plagues will come during the interval of about one year between the close of Christ's priestly work and His second coming.

Those who are obedient to God and who trust wholly in Jesus will be protected during all these plagues (Ps. 46:1–3; 91:7–10; Rev. 3:10; Joel 3:16). The only way we can hope to escape the plagues and have the protection of God during this terrible time is to turn to Him now in full obedience to all His commandments and the faith of Jesus (Rev. 14:12).

It will be too late to attempt to prepare when the first plague falls (Isa. 55:6). The decree of Revelation 22:11 will be pronounced by Christ before the first plague begins. No man knows when that decree will go forth.

The door of the ark closed seven days before the flood came (Gen. 7:1, 4, 16). All who were saved had to enter the ark on the seventh day before the flood began. So all who will be saved in this great coming world crisis will have to turn to God in obedience before Jesus closes the door of pardon and mercy before the seven plagues start. Sadly many will try in vain to enter when the door has been closed and it is forever too late (Luke 13:24–28). We need to be ready every day (2 Cor. 6:2; Jer. 8:20; Matt. 24:44).

The Second Coming of Jesus

There appears in the sky a cloud that betokens the coming of the King of kings and Lord of lords. In solemn silence God's people will gaze upon the cloud as it draws nearer and nearer to the earth. Brighter and brighter it will become, and more glorious, until it's a great white cloud, its glory as a consuming fire. Jesus rides forth as a mighty conqueror. "And the armies which were in heaven" follow Him (Rev. 19:14). The whole heaven seems filled with dazzling forms—"ten thousand times ten thousand, and thousands of thousands." No pen can describe it. No human mind is adequate to imagine the fantastic and holy scene. As the living cloud comes still nearer, every eye will behold the lovely Jesus. There's no crown of thorns on that holy brow, but now a crown of glory rests upon His sacred head. His face outshines the dazzling brightness of the sun.

"And he hath on his vesture and on his thigh a name written, King of Kings, and Lord of Lords" (Rev. 19:16). As the King of glory descends on the cloud amid terrific majesty, and wrapped in flaming fire, the earth trembles. The ground heaves and swells, and the very mountains move from their foundations. "Our God shall come, and shall not keep silence: a fire shall devour before him, and it shall be very tempestuous round about him. He shall call to the heavens from above, and to the earth, that he may judge his people" (Ps. 50:3, 4). "And the kings of the earth, and the great men, and the rich men, and the chief captains, and the mighty men, and every bondman, and every free man, hid themselves in the dens and in the rocks of the mountains; and said to the mountains and rocks, Fall on us, and hide us from the face of him that sitteth on the throne, and from the wrath of the Lamb: for the great day of his wrath is come; and who shall be able to stand?" (Rev. 6:15–17).

The jokes have stopped. Cursing, lying lips are now silent. In the middle of their terror the wicked hear the voices of God's people joyfully exclaiming: "Lo, this is our God; we have waited for him, and he will save us" (Isa. 25:9).

While the earth is reeling like a drunkard, amid the terrific roar of thunder and upheavals of nature, the voice of the Son of God calls His faithful ones of all ages from the grave. "For the Lord himself shall descend from heaven with a shout, with the voice of the archangel, and with the trump of God: and the dead in Christ shall rise first: Then we which are alive and remain shall be caught up together with them in the clouds, to meet the Lord in the air: and so shall we ever be with the Lord" (1 Thess. 4:16, 17). God's living people are changed "in a moment, in the twinkling of an eye" (1 Cor. 15:51). Those who have been raised from the four corners of the earth and the living who have just been changed are "caught up ... to meet the Lord in the air" (1 Thess. 4:16). Angels "gather together his elect from the four winds, from one end of heaven to the other" (Matt. 24:31). Little children who had died now live and are carried by holy angels to their mother's arms. Friends long separated by death are united, nevermore to part, and with songs of gladness ascend together to the city of God.

At the coming of Christ the wicked are destroyed by the brightness of His glory. Christ takes His people to the city of God, and the whole earth is emptied of its inhabitants—it becomes a desolate wilderness.

The following verses offer additional promises regarding Christ's return: John 14:1–3; Revelation 1:7; Matthew 24:27–31; 25:31; and Philippians 3:20, 21.

The New Jerusalem

For the first 1,000 years in heaven, I just want to walk upon the blissful shore holding my Saviors nail-pierced hand and gazing upon His lovely face.

At the close of the thousand years the second resurrection will take place. Then the wicked will be raised from the dead and appear before God for the execution of judgment. John the revelator, after describing the resurrection of the righteous, says, "The rest of the dead lived not again until the thousand years were finished" (Rev. 20:5).

Christ descends upon the Mount of Olives whence after His resurrection He ascended and where angels repeated the promise of His return. Says the prophet, "The Lord my God shall come, and all the saints with thee" (Zech. 14:5). And His feet shall stand in that day upon the Mount of Olives, which is before Jerusalem on the east, and the Mount of Olives shall cleave in the midst thereof and there shall be a very great valley.

As the New Jerusalem, in its dazzling splendor comes down out of heaven, it rests upon the place purified and made ready to receive it, and Christ with His people and the angels enter the Holy City (Zech. 14:4–9).

These verses are also comforting: Isaiah 60:19, 20; John 14:2; Galatians 4:26; Revelation 21:2; and 22:5.

Hell Fire

After the thousand years God raises up the wicked people. In the vast throng are multitudes of races that existed before the flood. Men of lofty stature and giant intellect who yielded to the control of fallen angels and made God's law null and void are now gathered together. Satan marshals an army to lay their plans to take possession of the riches and glory of the New Jerusalem.

"Upon the wicked he shall rain snares, fire and brimstone, and an horrible tempest: this shall be a portion of their cup" (Ps. 11:6). "Fire comes down from God out of heaven. The earth is broken up. The weapons concealed in its depths are drawn forth. Devouring flames burst from every yawning chasm. The very rocks are on fire. The day has come that shall burn as an oven. The elements melt with fervent heat, the earth also, and the works that are therein are burned up" (*Maranatha,* p. 348).

The earth's surface seems to be one molten mass—a vast seething lake of fire. The wicked receive their recompenses in the earth. Satan's punishment is to be far greater than those of whom he has deceived. In the cleansing flames, the wicked are at last destroyed—root and branch: Satan the root, his followers the branches. The full penalty of the law has been visited. The demands of justice have been met, and heaven and earth beholding, declare the righteousness of Jehovah. Read also Isaiah 9:5; 34:2, 8; Psalms 11:6; and Malachi 4:1.

Eden Restored

"And I saw a new heaven and a new earth: for the first heaven and the first earth were passed away" (Rev. 21:1). The fire that consumes the wicked purifies the earth. Every trace of the curse is swept away. But no eternally burning hell will exist; the earth will be cleansed once and for all (Rev. 20:6; Isa. 45:18; Ps. 37:29; 84:11; Micah 4:8; Eph. 1:14).

One of my greatest joys is found in Isaiah 66:22, 23: "For as in the new heavens and the new earth, which I will make, shall remain before me, saith the Lord, so shall your seed and your name remain. And it shall come to pass, that from one new moon to another, and from one sabbath to another, shall all flesh come to worship before me, saith the Lord."

And we shall hear the angel choir, but most of all we shall hear God sing for us. God's people, so long pilgrims and wanderers, shall find a home. "My people shall dwell in a peaceable habitation, and in sure dwellings, and in quiet resting places" (Isa. 32:18). Violence shall no more be heard in the land, wasting nor destruction within its borders.

"They shall build houses, and inhabit them; and they shall plant vineyards, and eat the fruit of them. They shall not build, and another inhabit; they shall not plant, and another eat ... mine elect shall long enjoy the work of their hands" (Isa. 65:22).

"The wolf also shall dwell with the lamb, and the leopard shall lie down with the kid ... and a little child shall lead them.... They shall not hurt nor destroy in all my holy mountain," saith the Lord (Isa. 11:6, 9).

There will be no more tears, no funeral trains, no badges of mourning. There shall be no more death, neither sorrow, nor crying. The New Jerusalem is the metropolis of the glorified new earth. "The tabernacle of God is with men, and he will dwell with them, and they shall be his people, and God himself shall be with them, and be their God" (Rev. 21:3).

Clothed in immortality, we will wing our flight to worlds afar. With unutterable delight we shall enter into the joy and the wisdom of unfallen beings. *And through endless ages, I will tell my story of how the wondrous cross led me home.*

For additional reading, look up 1 Corinthians 2:9; Isaiah 11:6, 9; 32:18; 60:18; 65:19–22; and Hebrews 11:14–16

Chapter 18

My Story

Though the rebel of old fought the storms of life and is battle scarred, I am at peace. I'm in the last chapter of my life, and I do not know how long the Lord will spare me. I am assured of a place in God's kingdom because I have made my calling and election sure. Every morning I drink deeply from the fountain of life, God's Word, which satisfies and quenches my hunger and thirst. My God has brought me through many trials and tribulations. Now I bask in the Savior's love. I am tired of this gloomy world and pine for my heavenly home. I await that great day.

After all these years my wife is still the rose of my life; she is my best friend and confidante. Our girls are well-educated women now who are strong in their faith and love the Lord. We are so proud of them. We taught them Christian values. We never ceased in our love, praise, encouragement, and support of them, forging a family bond that can never be broken. They have blessed us with adorable grandchildren who are our pride and joy. We have the best sons-in-law one could wish for—decent, upright, and respectful.

A long time ago I promised the Lord that I would write down my experiences and publish them. I kept on putting it off until tomorrow, but tomorrow never came. The months dragged into years until I got struck with incurable cancer.

The Lord clutched me from the jaws of death and restored me. I had enough time to contemplate life and realized that the Lord was not finished with me yet. The Lord will get *His* will done one way or the other. I was like a modern day Jonah.

While preparing this book, the Holy Spirit brought to my remembrance things long hidden in the dark recesses of my mind. I pray these stories will bring inspiration and encouragement into your life, and I hope you will have a closer walk with Jesus, for He is real!

We invite you to view the complete
selection of titles we publish at:

www.TEACHServices.com

Scan with your mobile
device to go directly
to our website.

Please write or email us your praises, reactions, or
thoughts about this or any other book we publish at:

TEACH Services, Inc.
P U B L I S H I N G
www.TEACHServices.com

P.O. Box 954
Ringgold, GA 30736

info@TEACHServices.com

TEACH Services, Inc., titles may be purchased in bulk for
educational, business, fund-raising, or sales promotional use.
For information, please e-mail:

BulkSales@TEACHServices.com

Finally, if you are interested in seeing
your own book in print, please contact us at

publishing@TEACHServices.com

We would be happy to review your manuscript for free.